The American Frontier
Coloring Book

A. K. Fielding

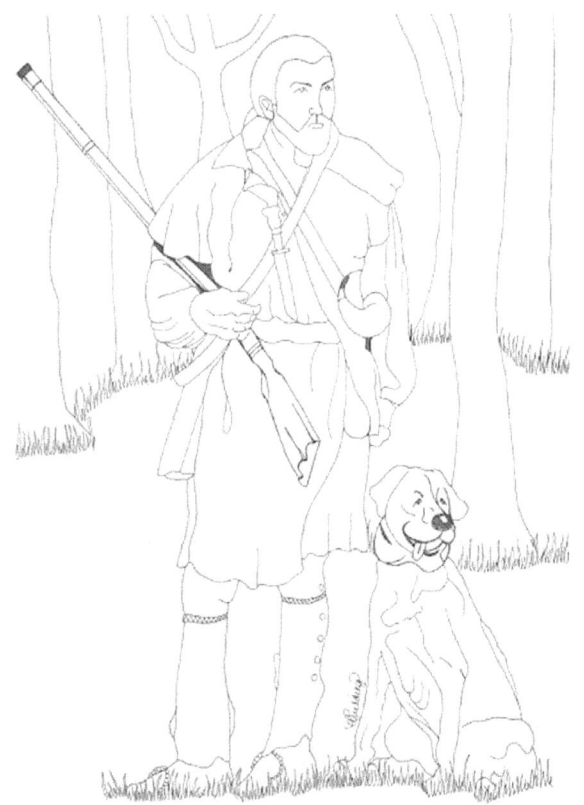

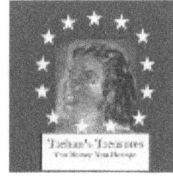

Trehan's Treasures Studio

http://www.trehanstreasures.com/

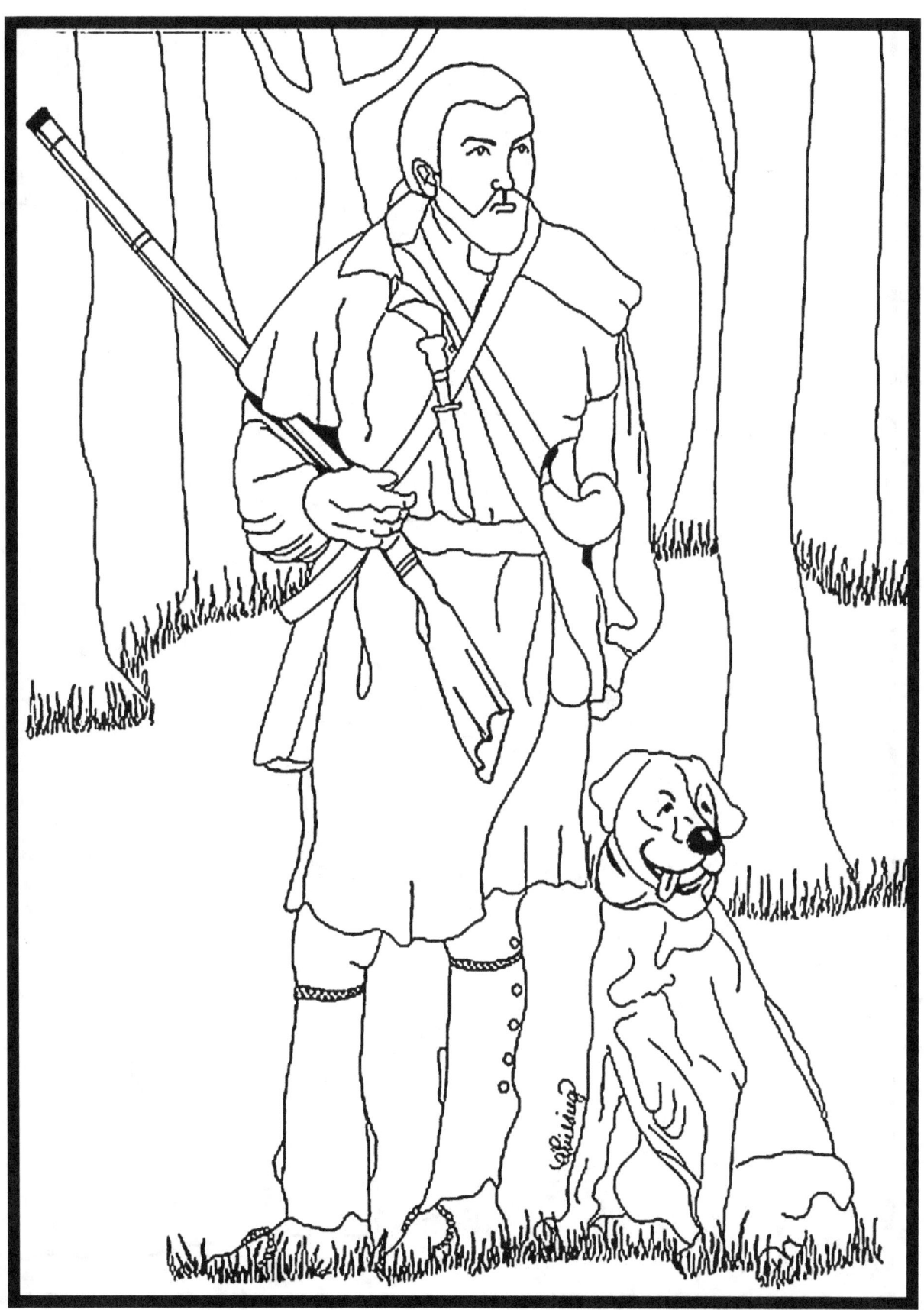

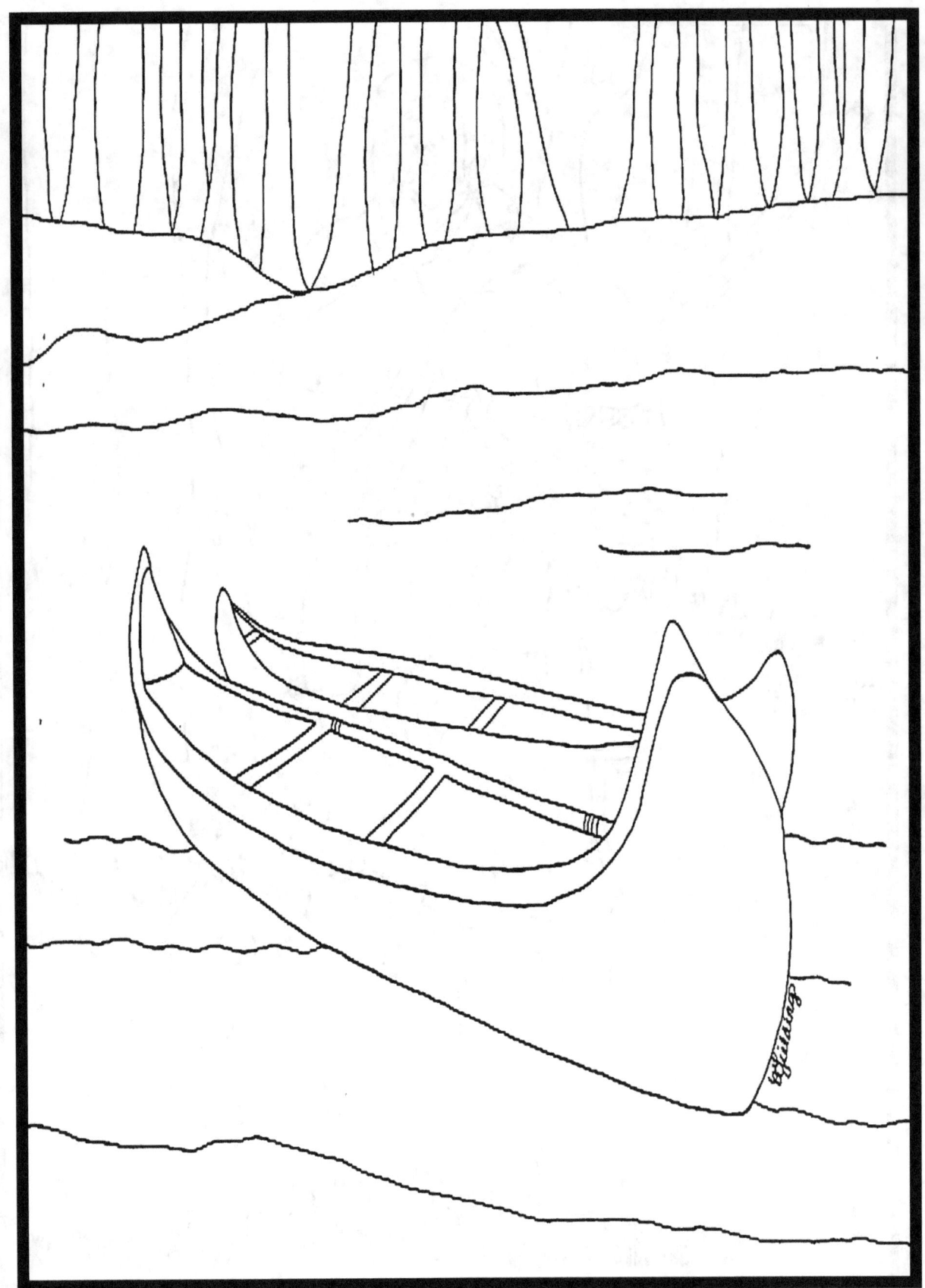

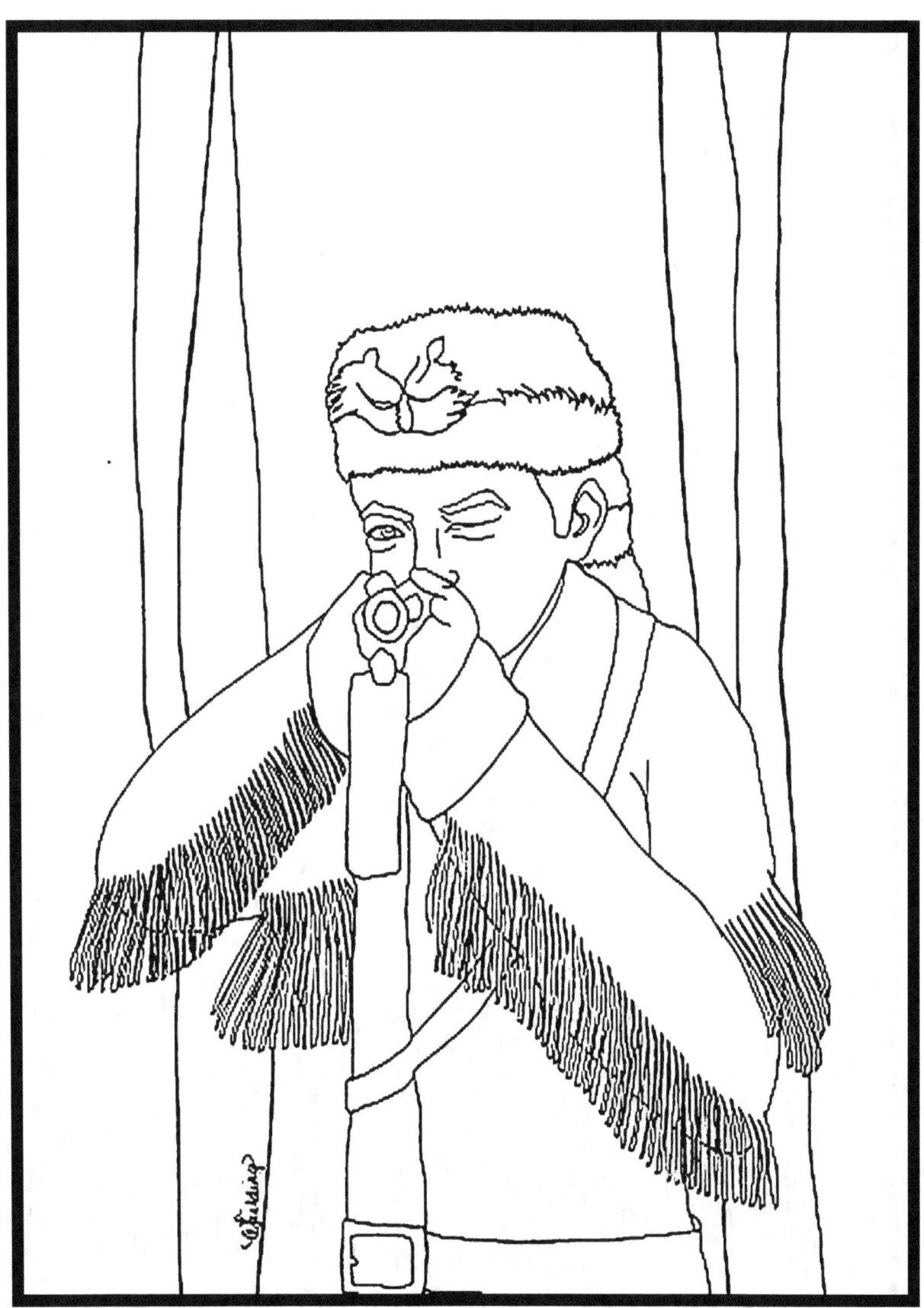

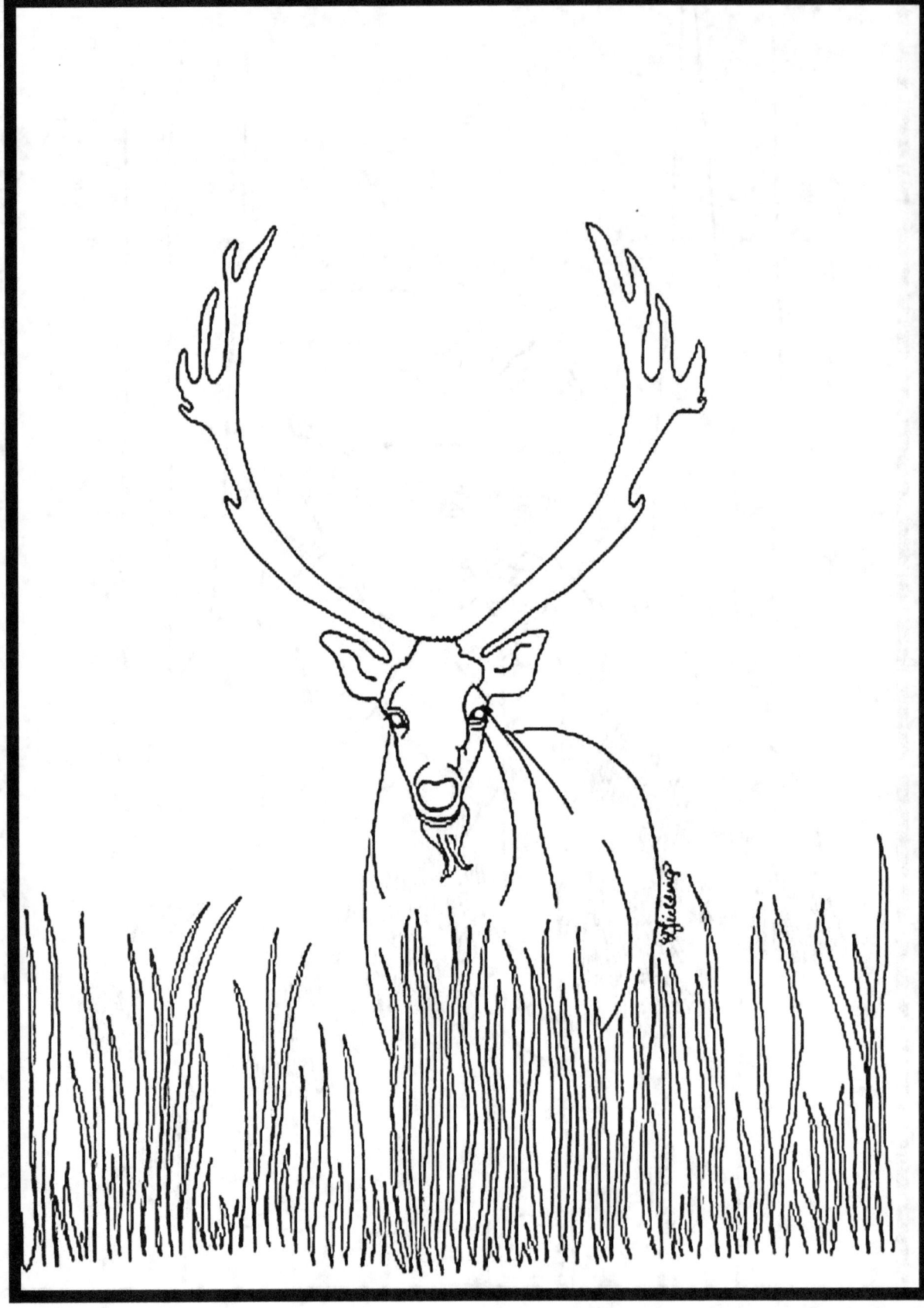

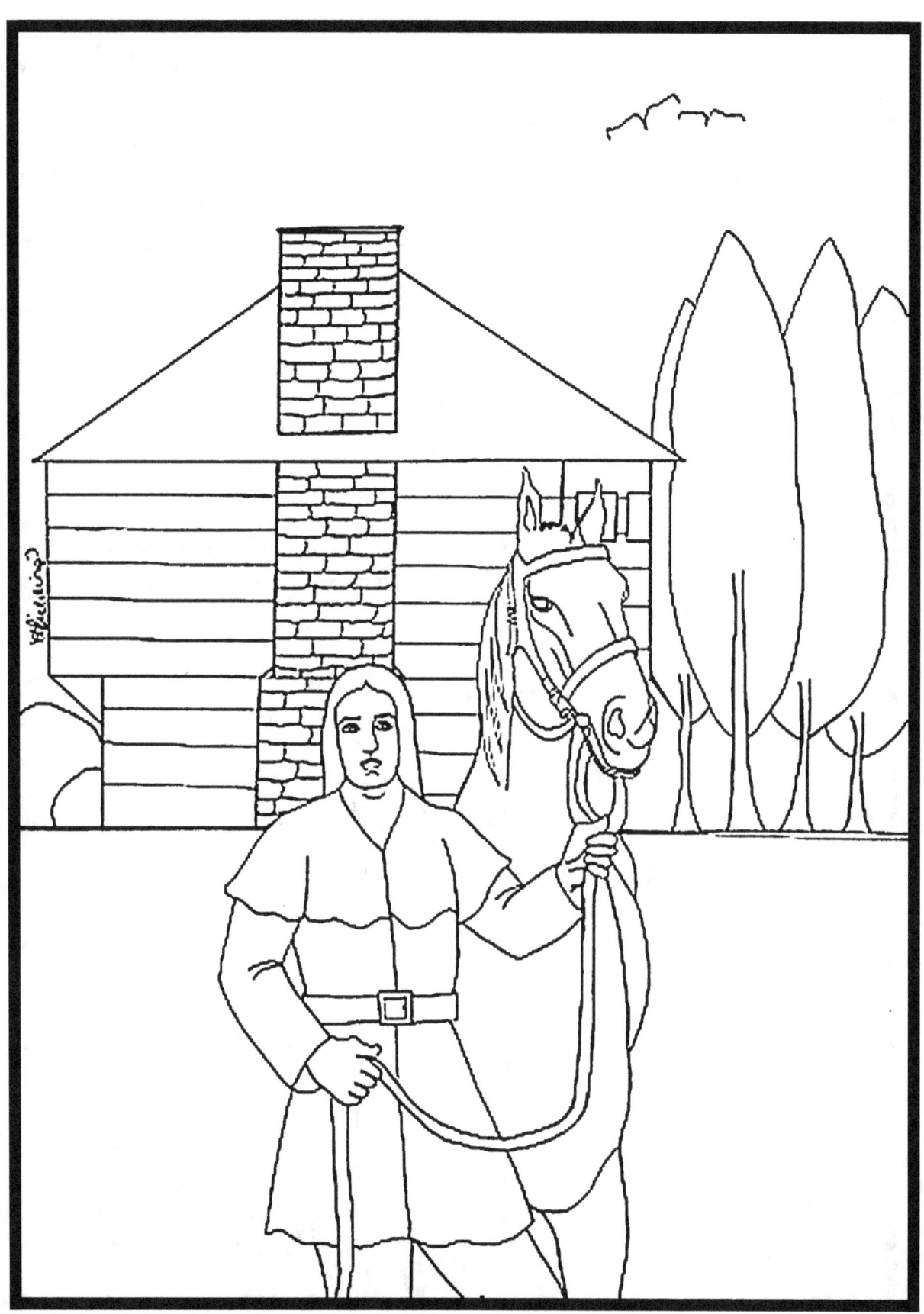

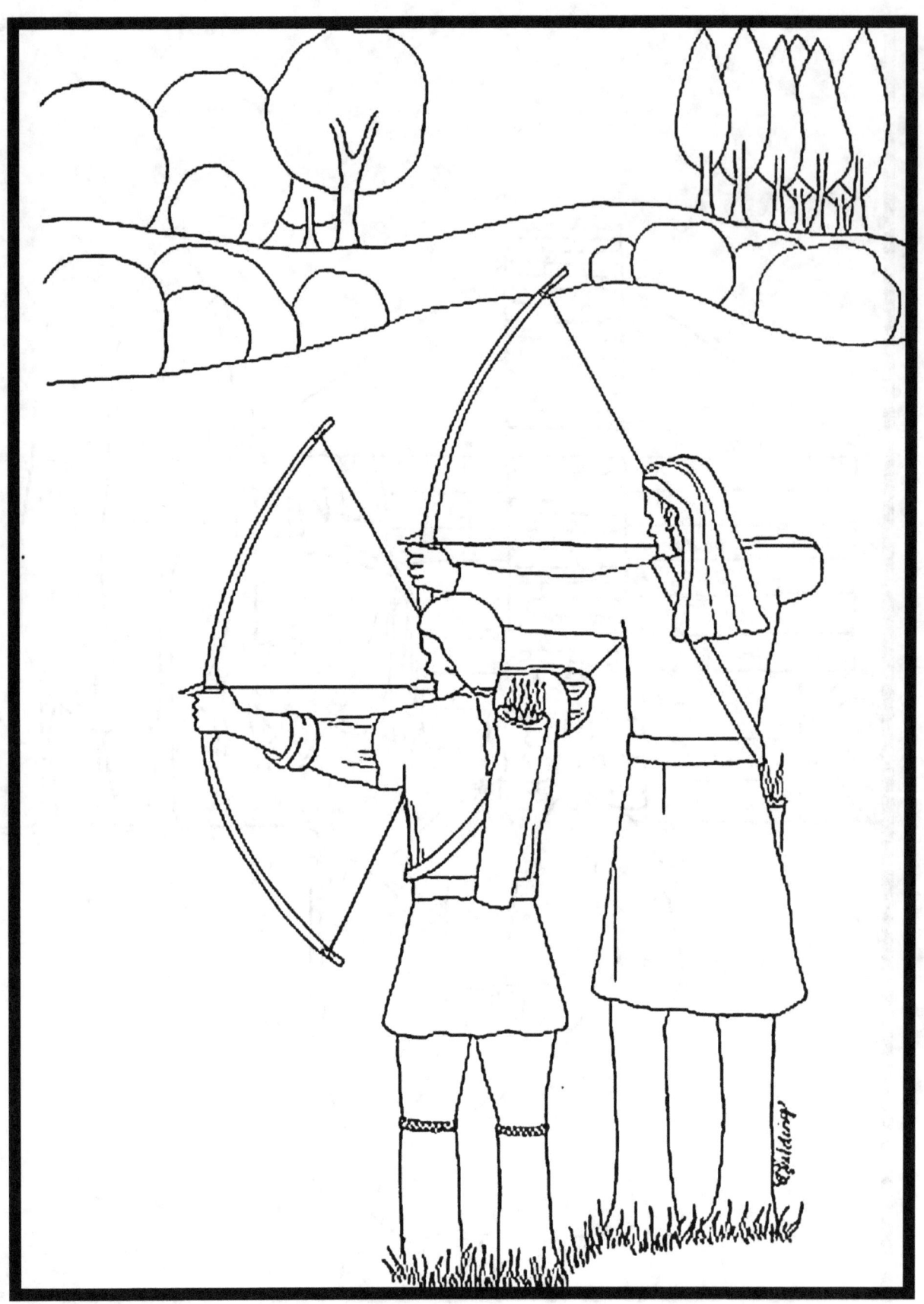

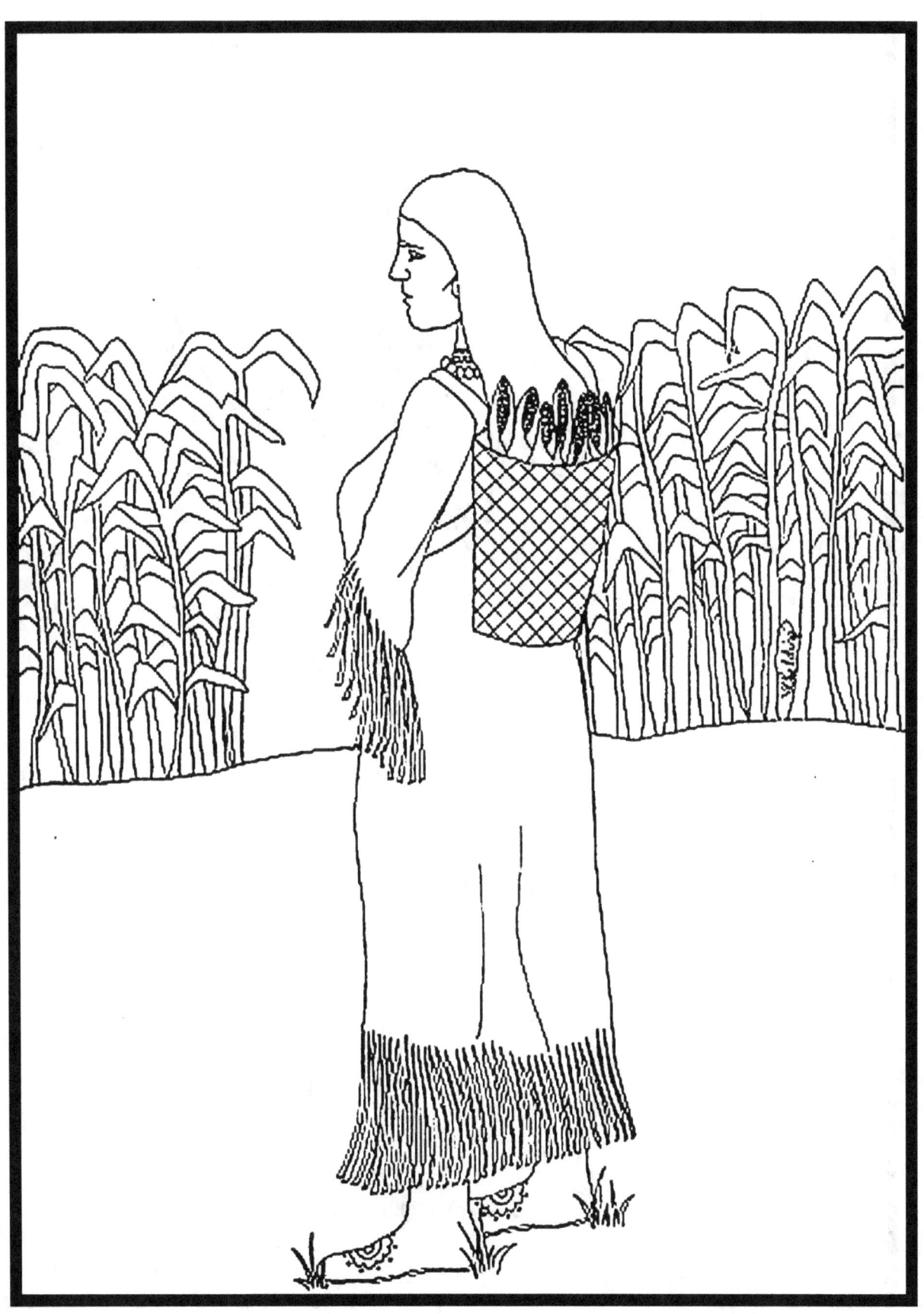

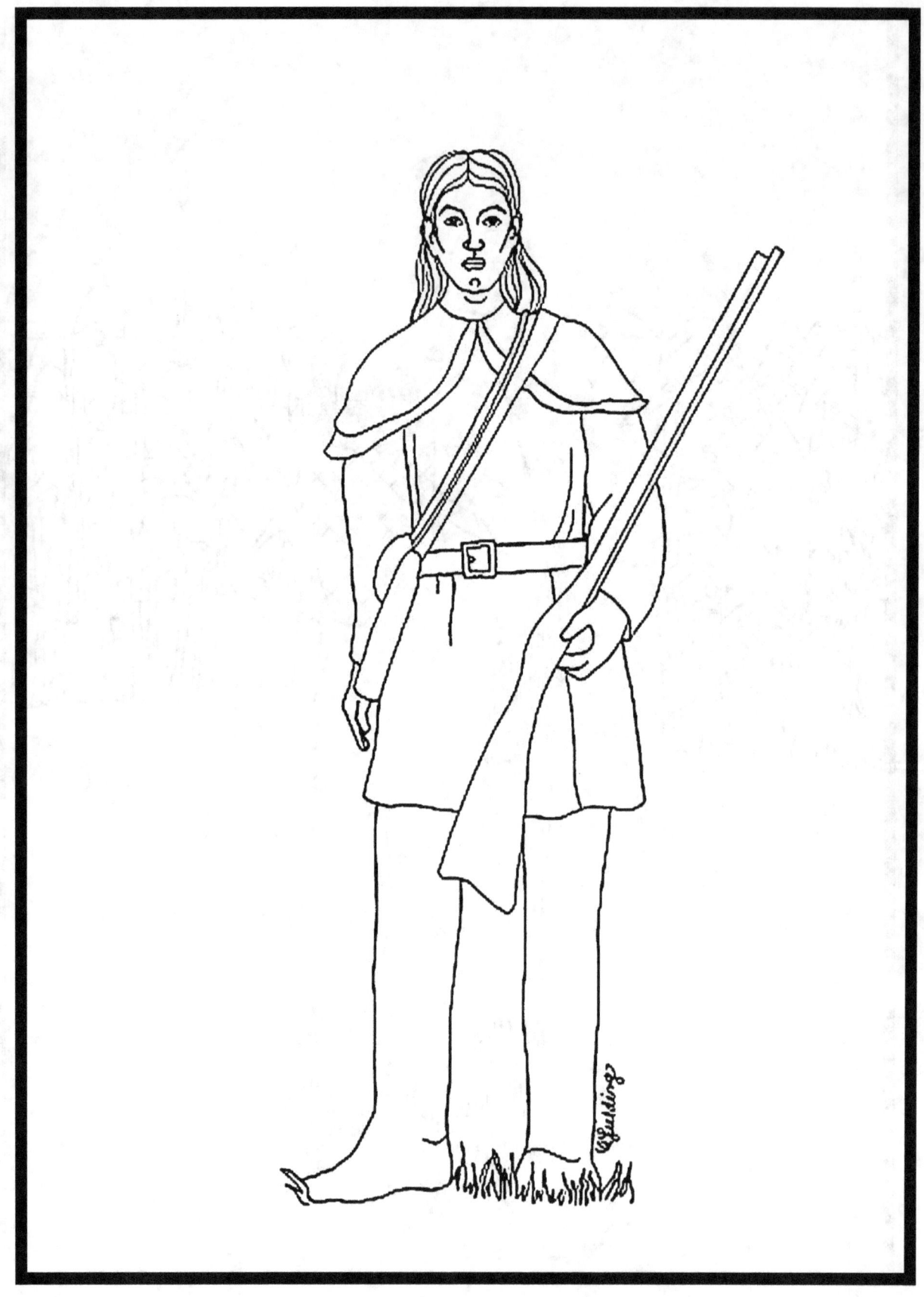

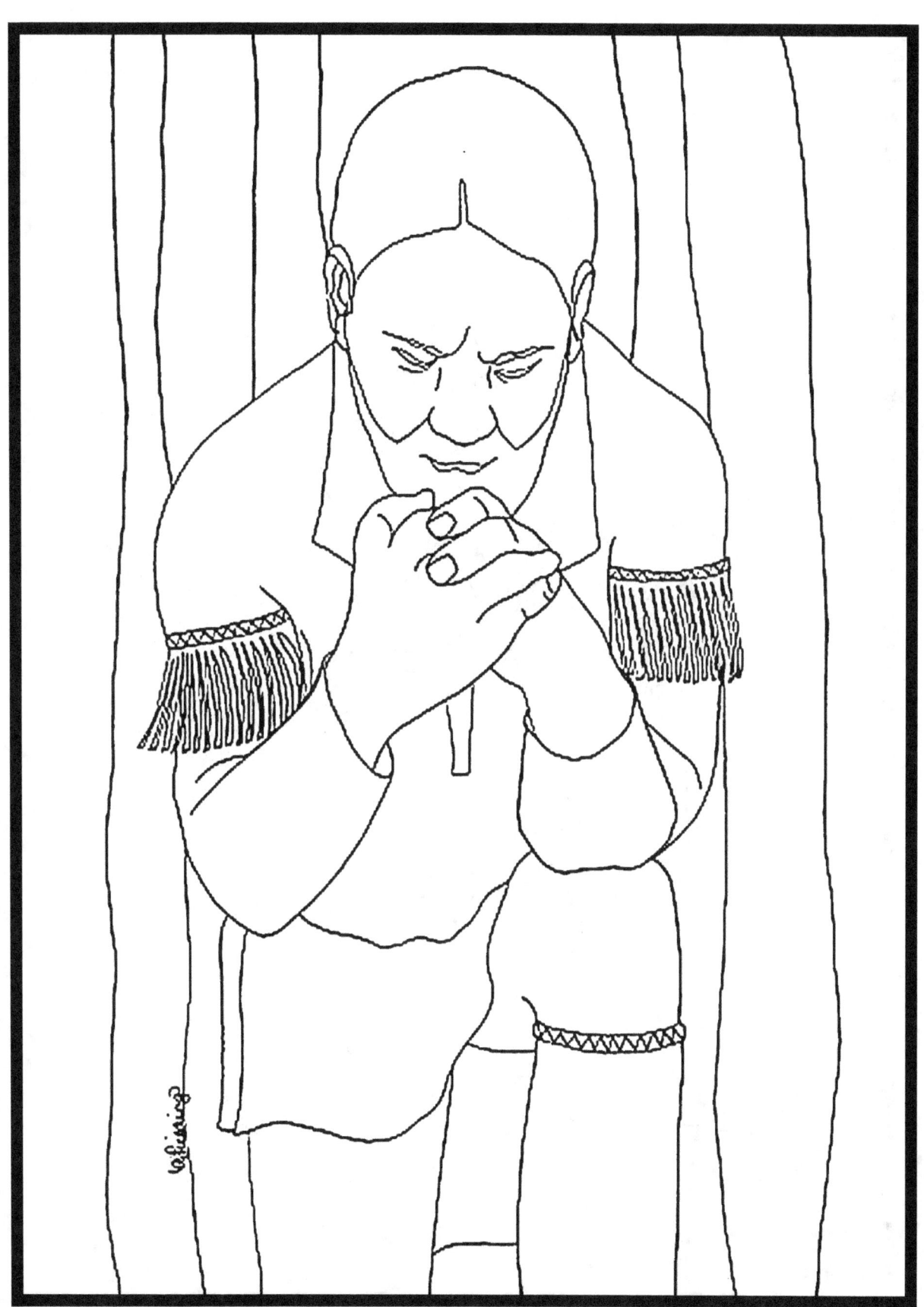

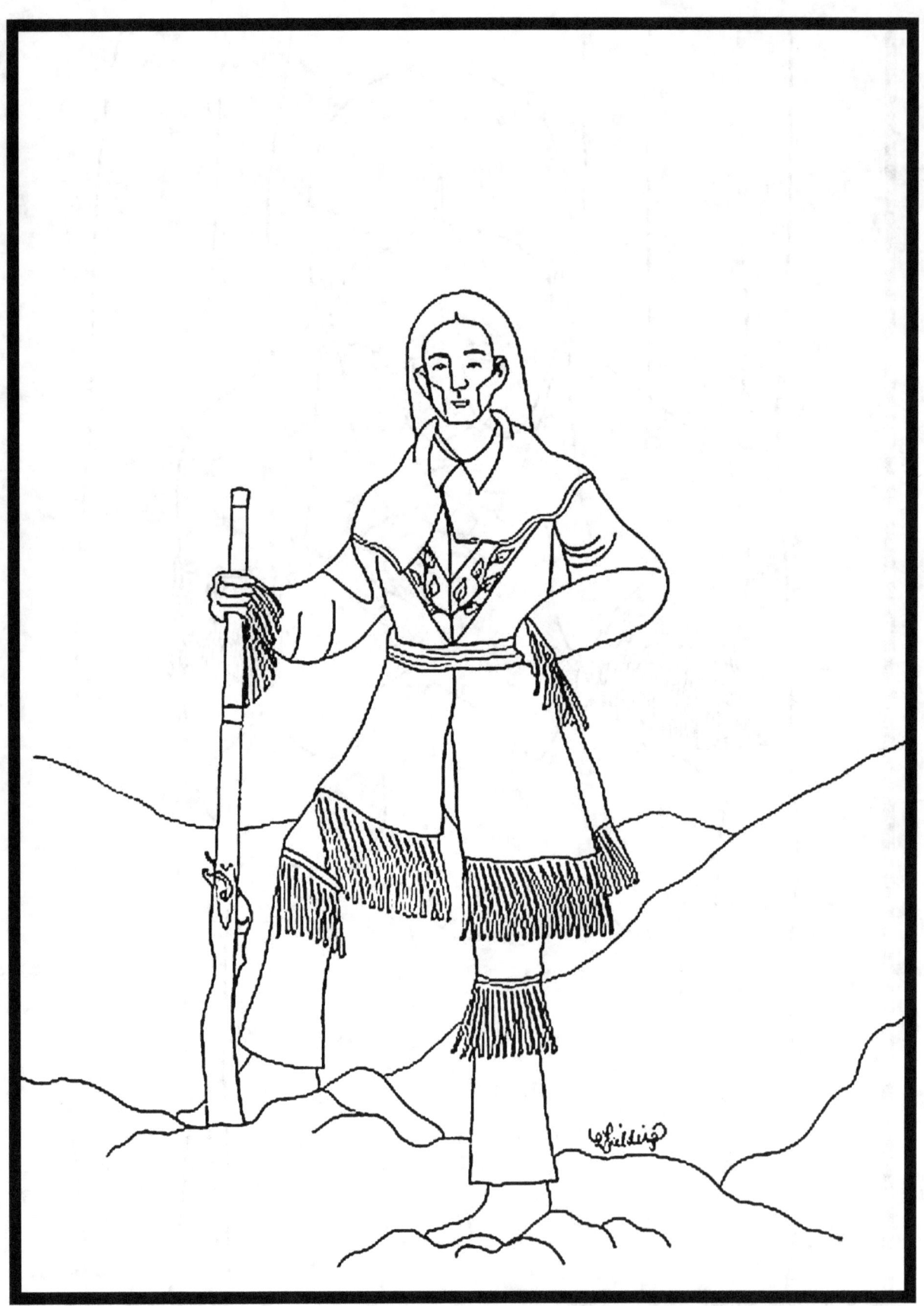

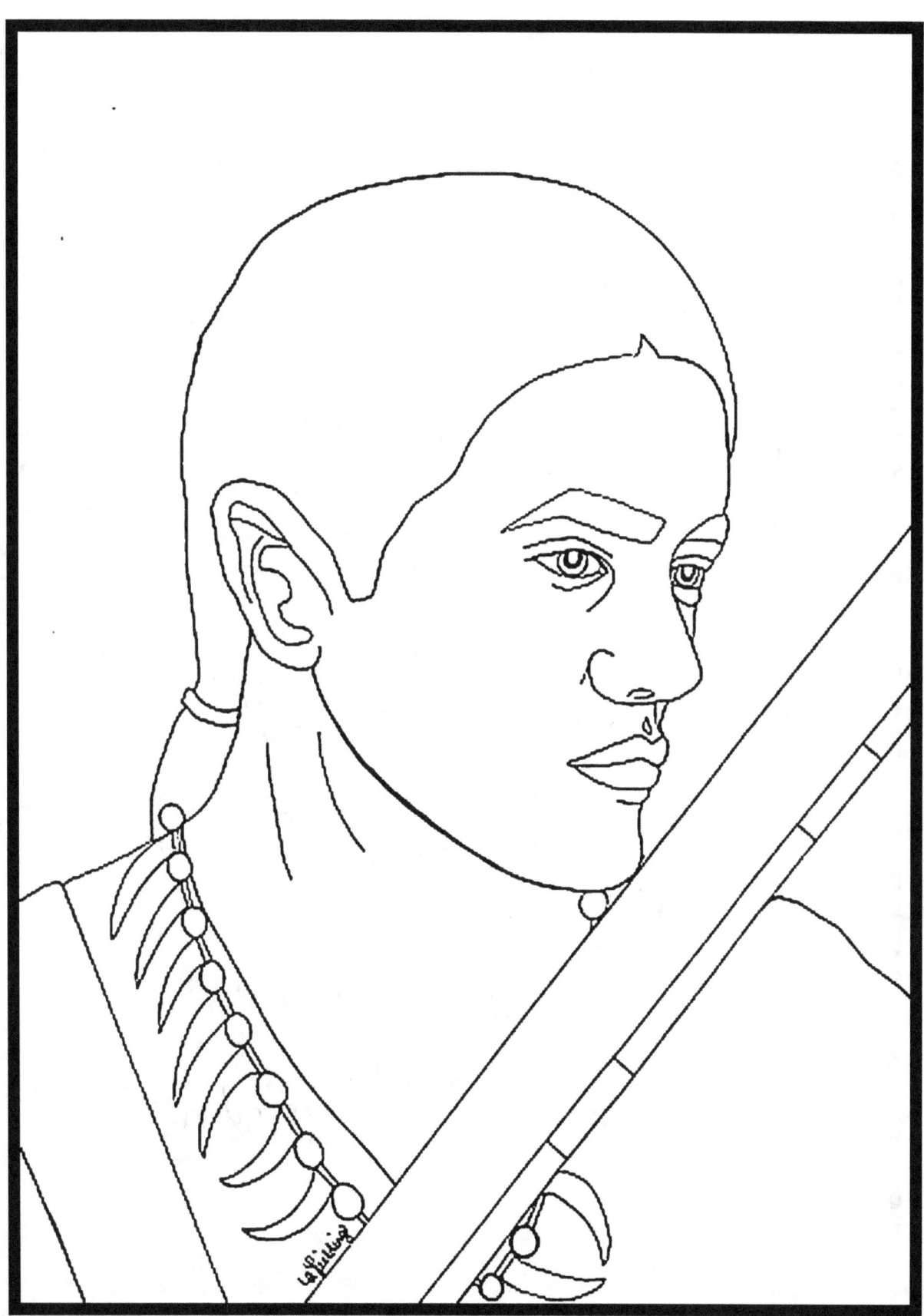

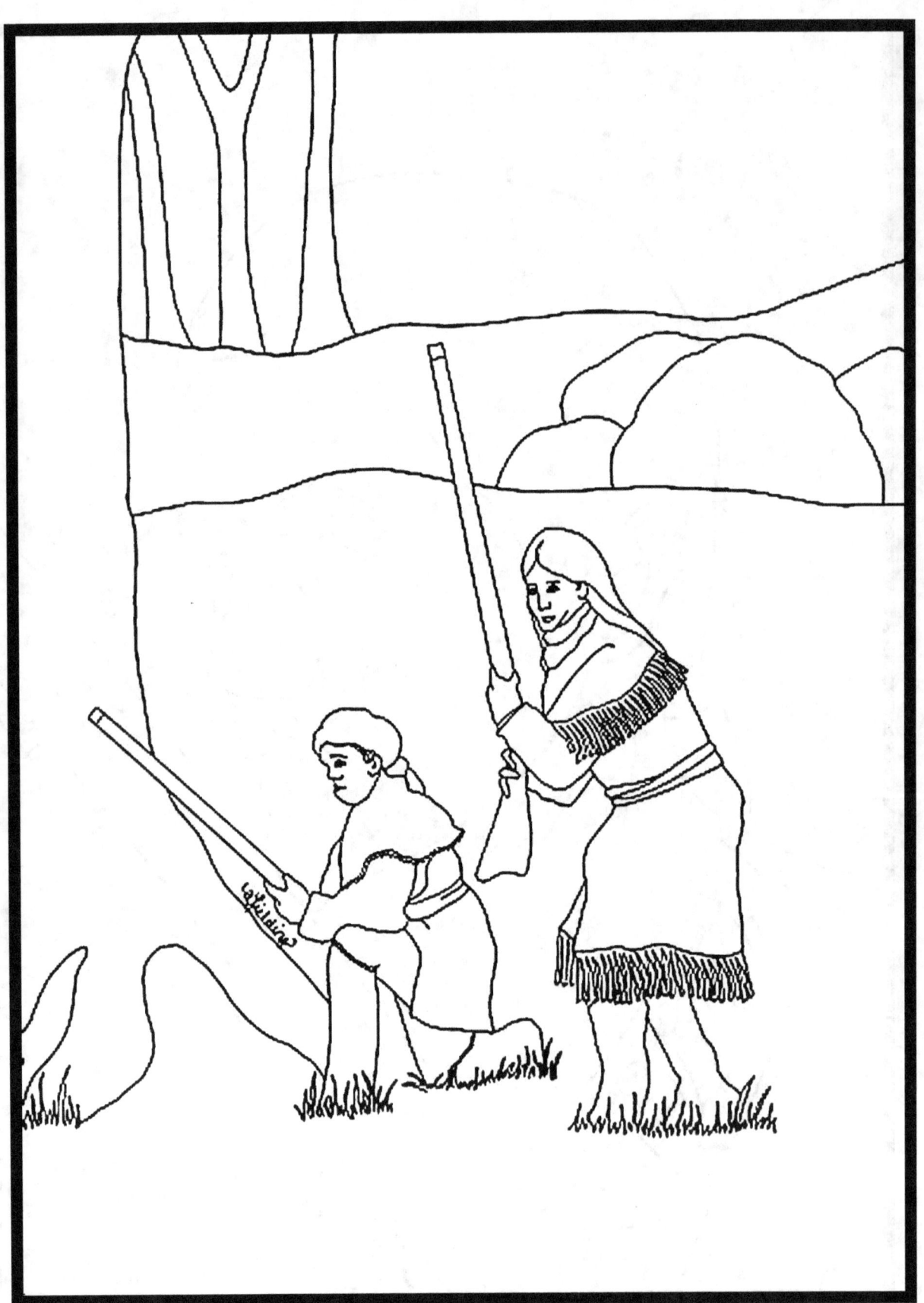

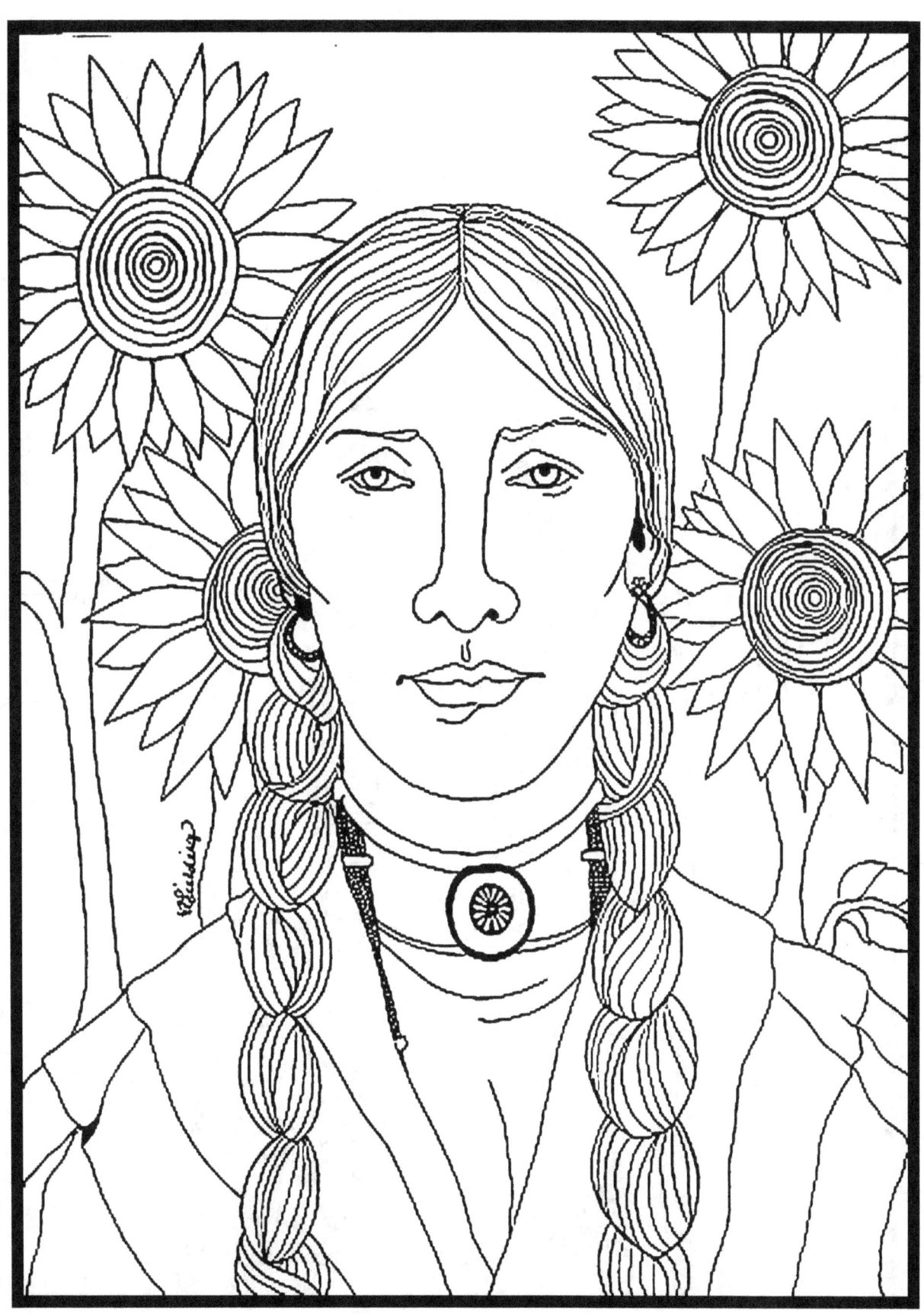

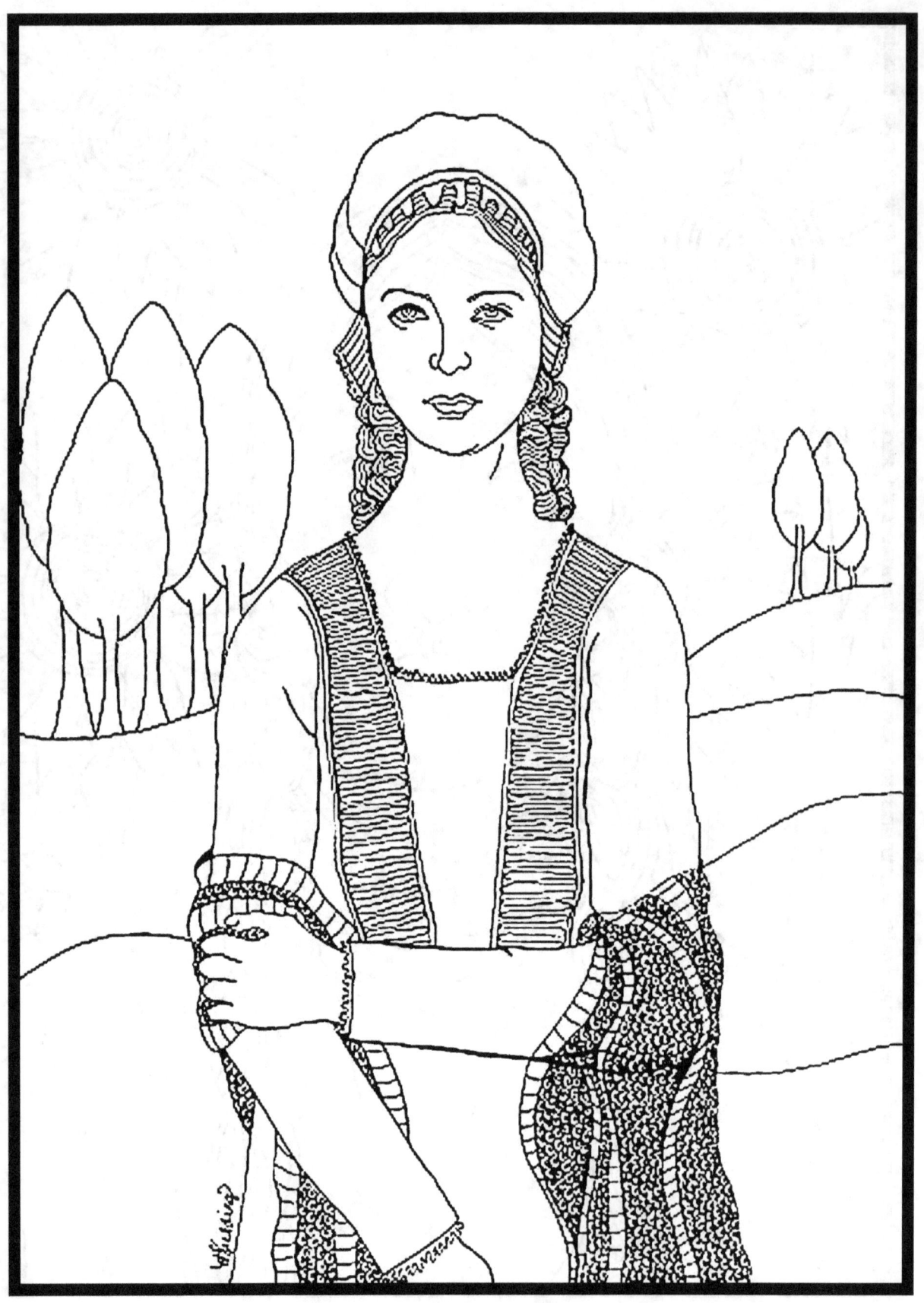

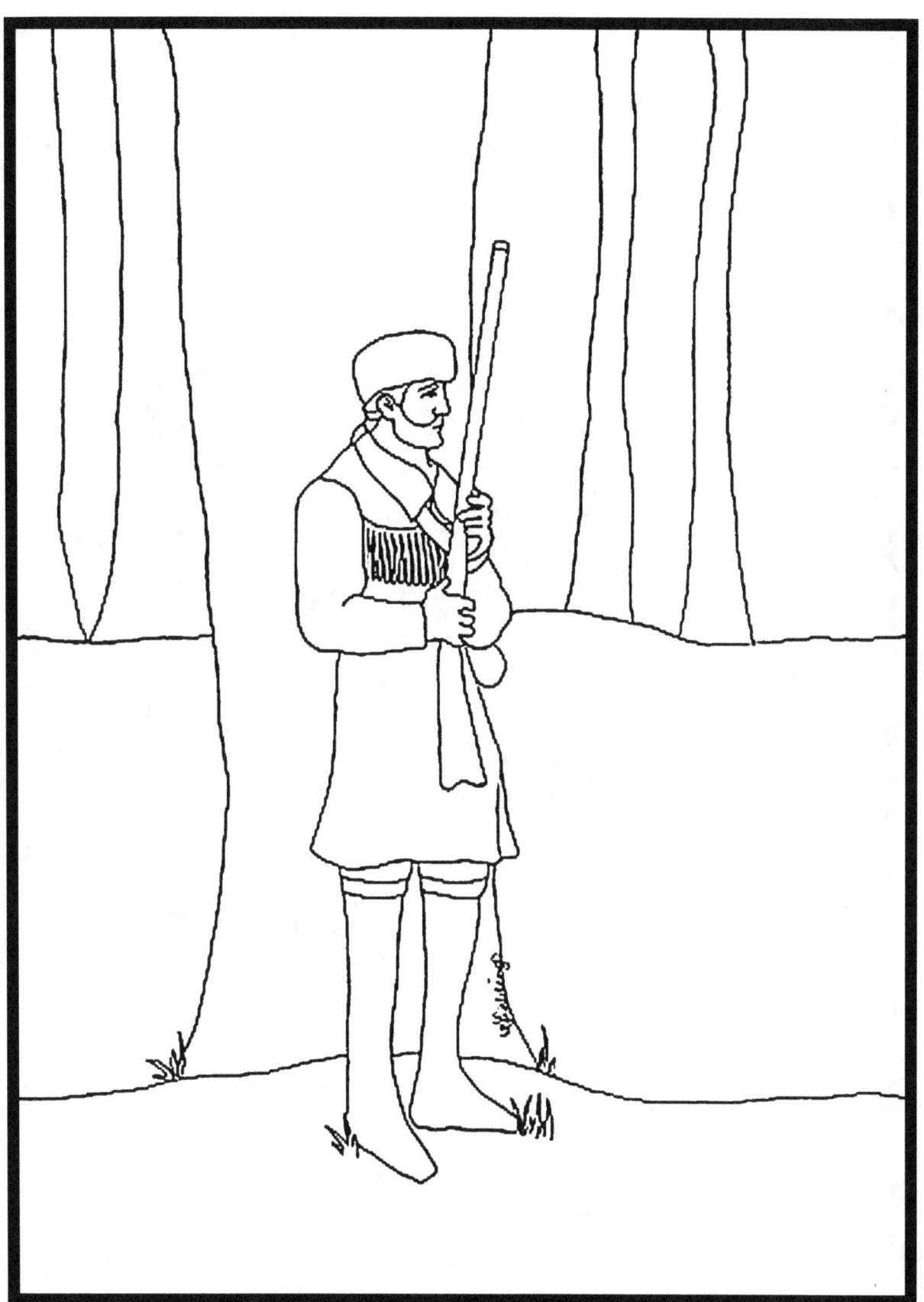

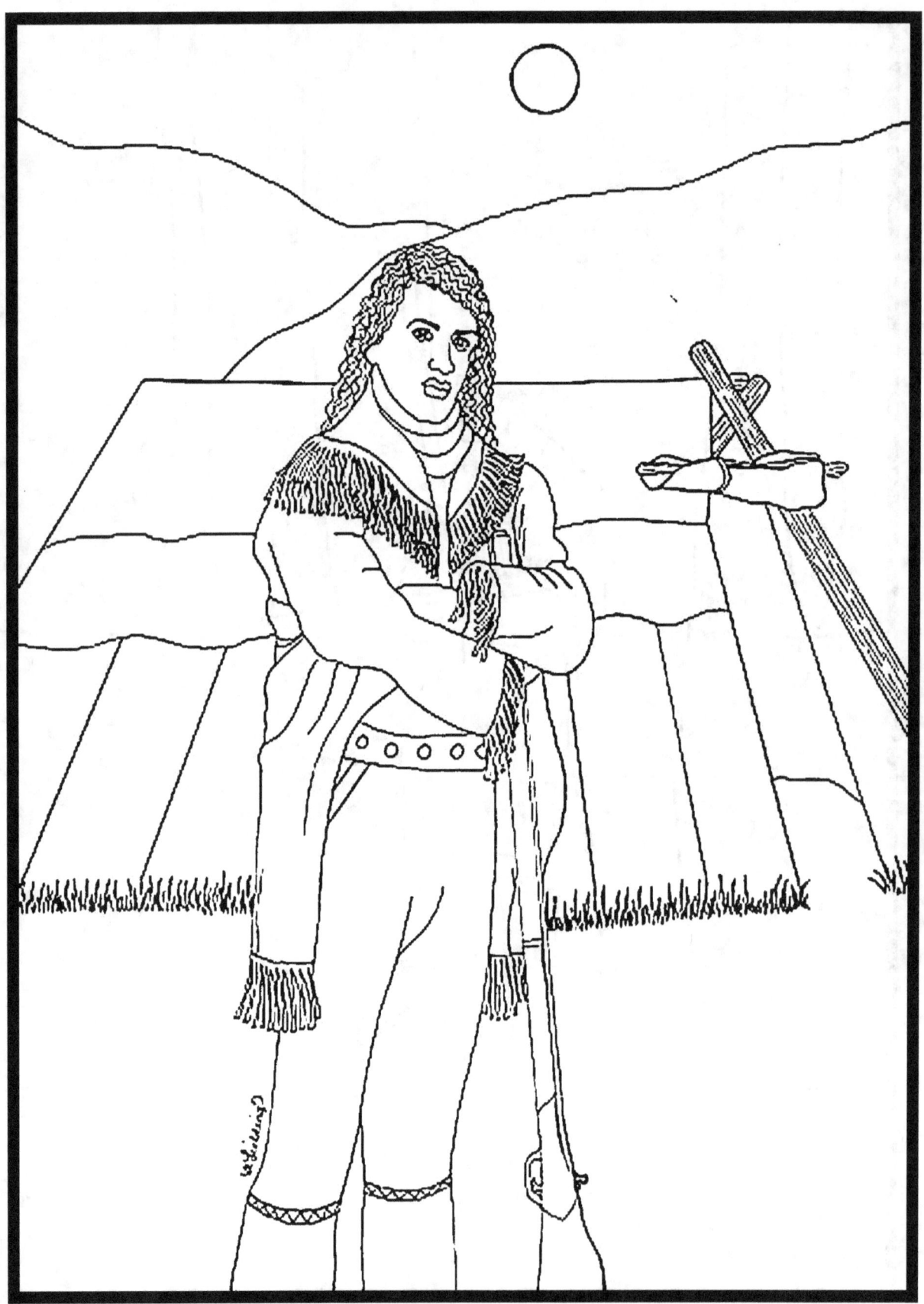

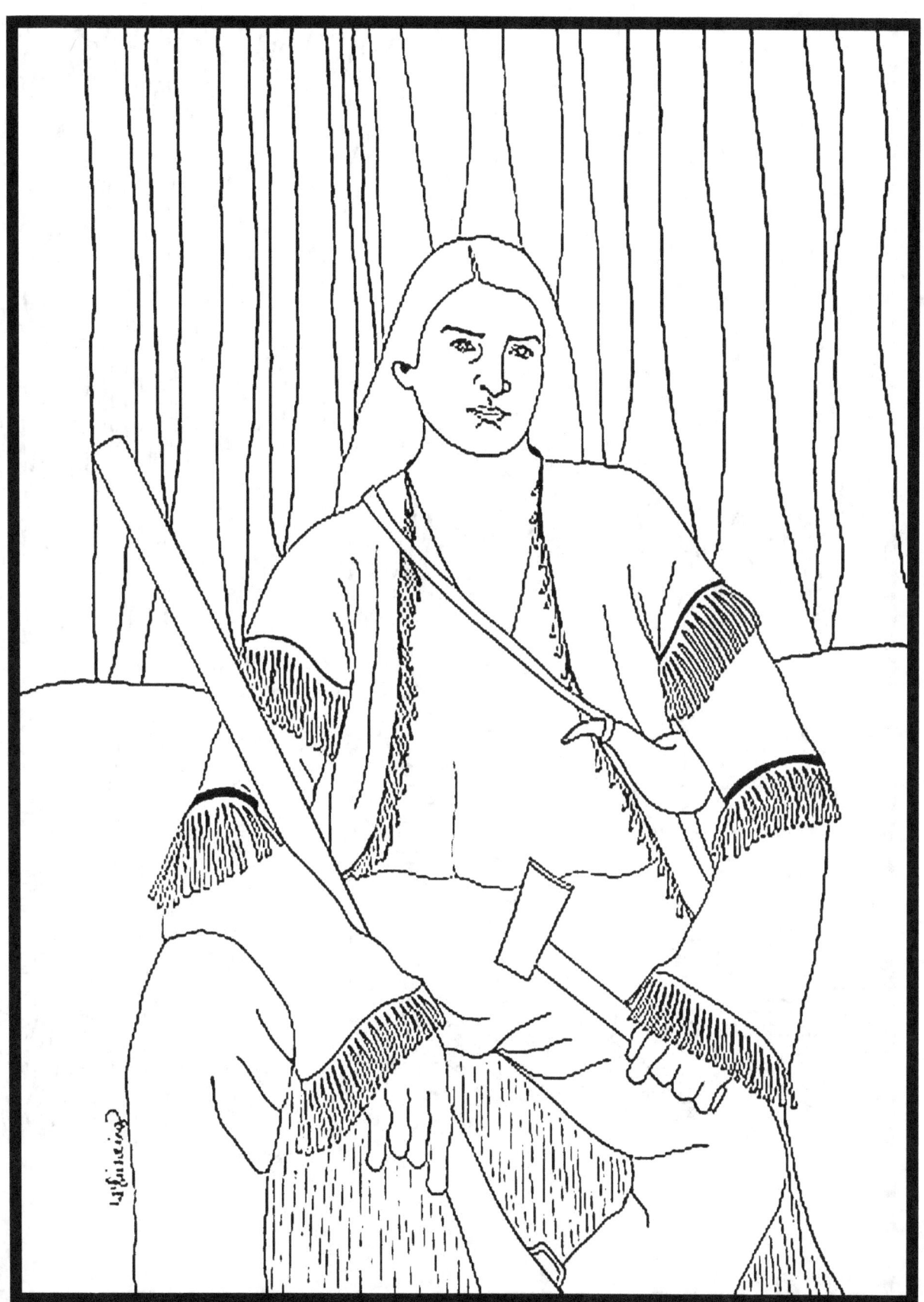

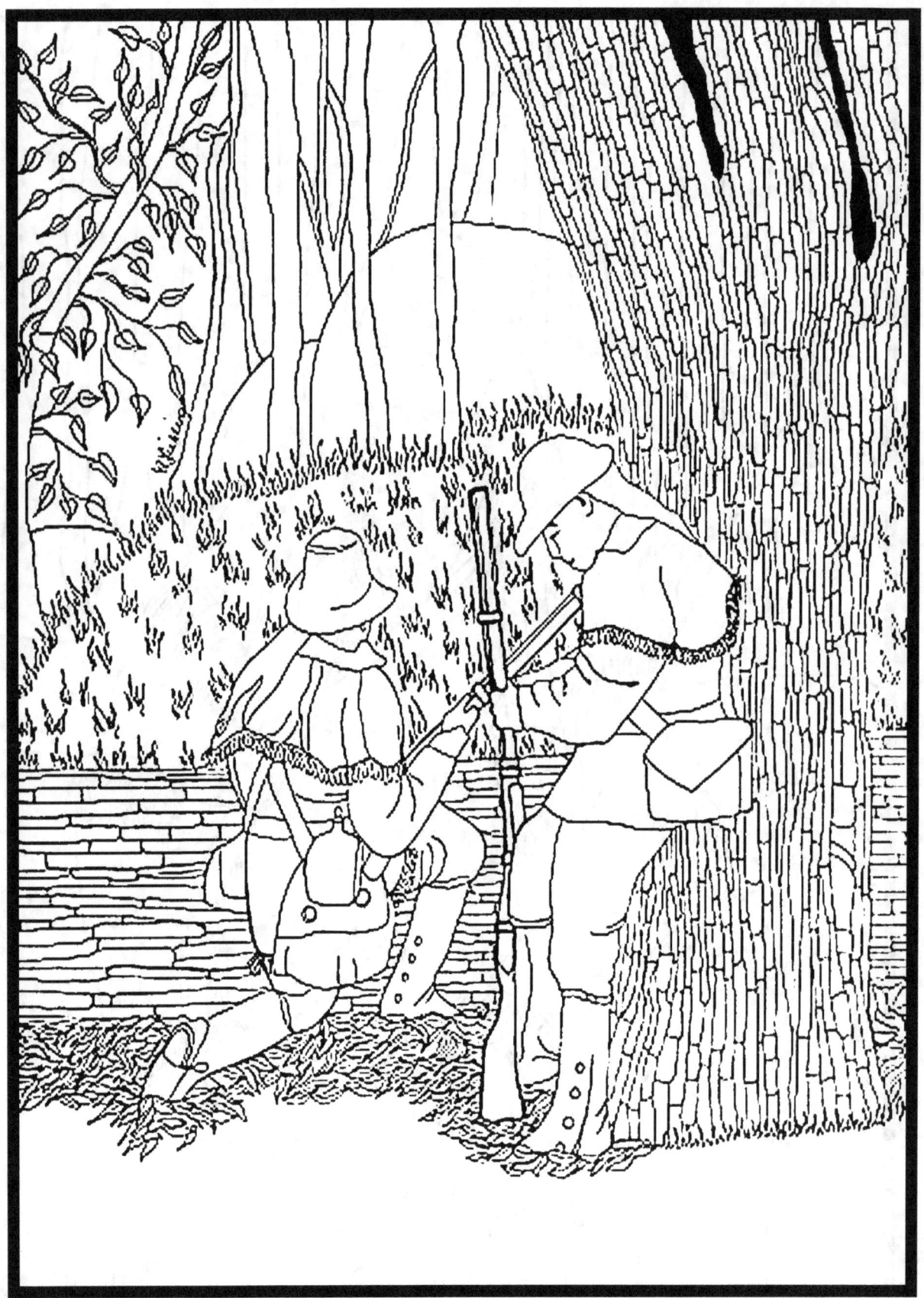

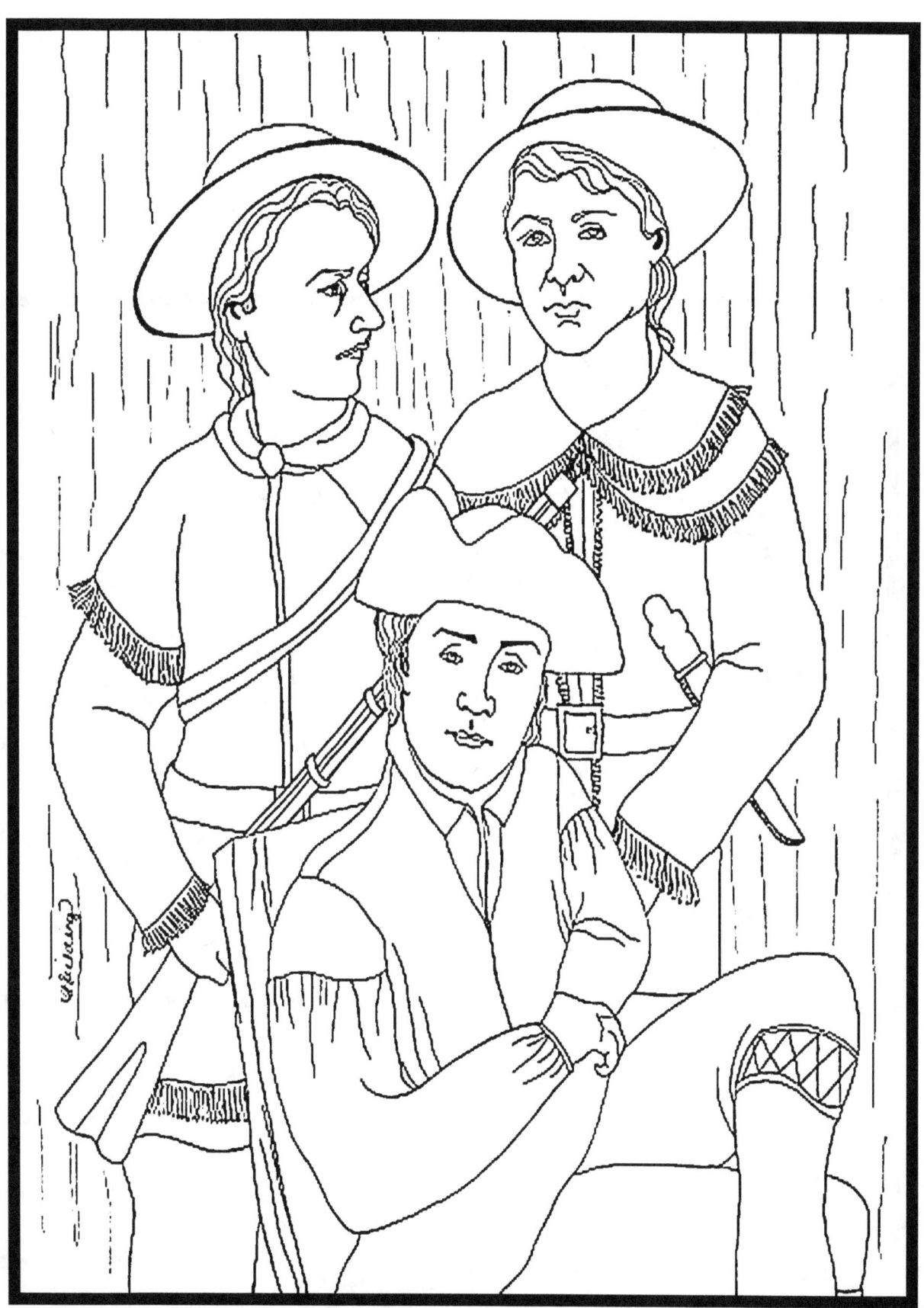

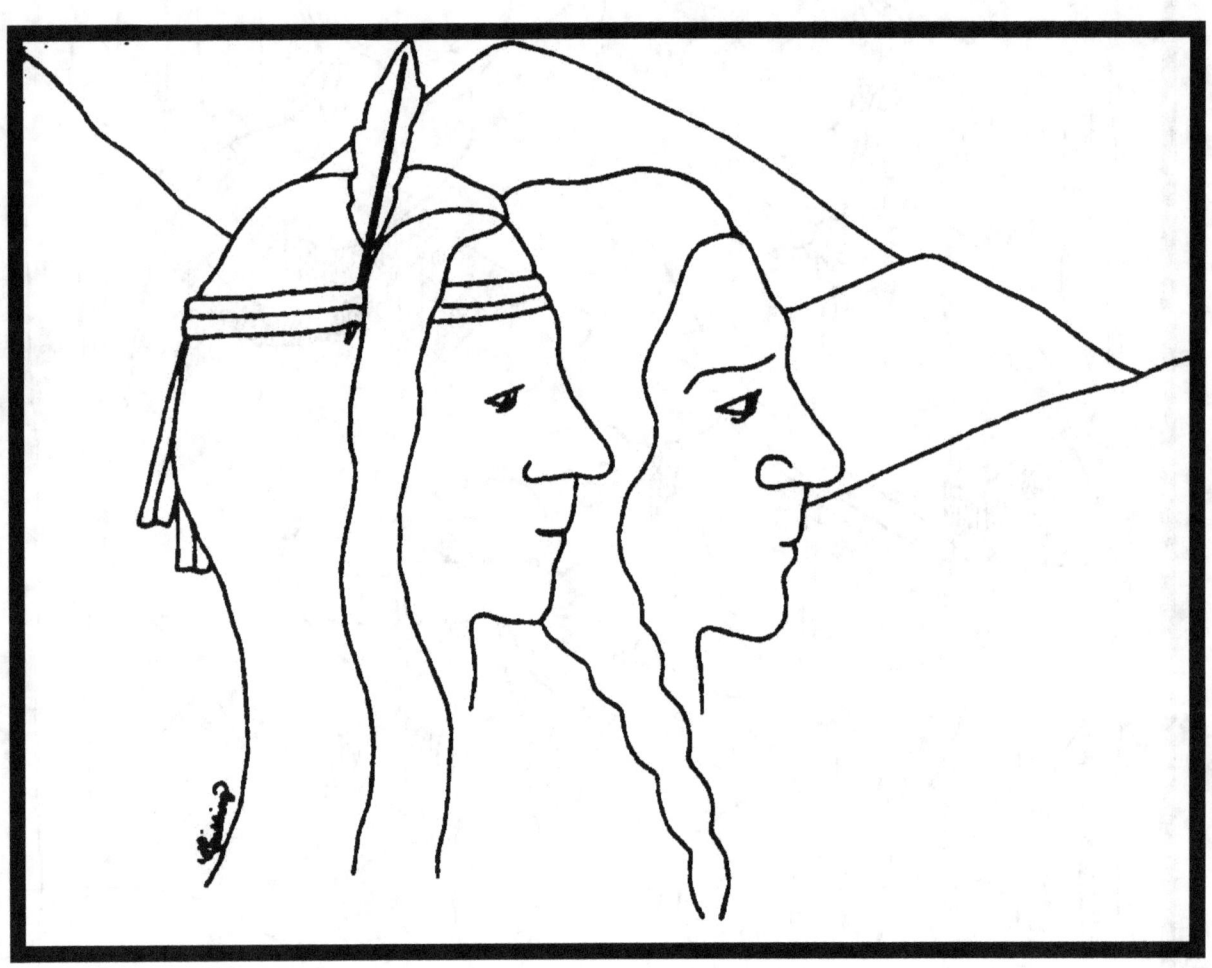

Other Books by A. K. Fielding

A Little Book of Revolutionary Quotes: God, Guns, & Government

A Little Book of Revolutionary Quotes: Tyranny, Taxes, & Treason

A Little Book of Revolutionary Quotes: Virtue, Valor, & Vice

Benjamin Franklin's *Poor Richard's Almanack* Illustrated

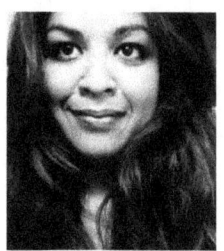

A.K. Fielding

For more news and information about

A. K. Fielding, please visit:

http://www.trehanstreasures.com/

www.ingramcontent.com/pod-product-compliance
Lightning Source LLC
Chambersburg PA
CBHW081424170526
45166CB00010B/3447